Mexico

Mexico

Sam and Beryl Epstein

A FIRST BOOK | REVISED EDITION
FRANKLIN WATTS
NEW YORK | LONDON | TORONTO | SYDNEY | 1983

FRONTISPIECE: A PRIMITIVE
EFFIGY VESSEL, FOUND IN VERACRUZ

Map courtesy of: Vantage Art, Inc.

Cover photograph of Chapala, Mexico,
courtesy of Taurus Photos (Fred West)

Photographs courtesy of:
The Metropolitan Museum of Art: opp. title page;
Mexican Government Tourism Office: pp. 3, 7, 10, 13, 28, 52, 56;
American Airlines: p. 16;
American Museum of Natural History: p. 21;
The United Nations: pp. 36, 39
(Food and Agriculture Organization photo by R. Coral), 48, 49;
Wide World Photos: p. 44.

Library of Congress Cataloging in Publication Data

Epstein, Sam, 1909-
Mexico.

(A First book)
Rev. ed. of: The first book of Mexico.
Rev. ed. [1967]
Includes index.
Summary: Presents an overview of Mexican history
and analyzes the country's pressing social
and economic problems, which include unequal
distribution of wealth and rapid population growth.
1. Mexico—Juvenile literature. [1. Mexico]
I. Epstein, Beryl Williams, 1910- . II. Title.
F1208.5.E6 1983   972   82-17452
ISBN 0-531-04530-7

Contents

Mexico

Mexico

UNITED STATES

Gulf of Mexico

YUCATAN

QUINTANA ROO

BELIZE

GUATEMALA

Candelaria R.

Papantla

Oaxaca

Teotihuacán

Xochimilco

Puebla

Cholula

Mexico City

Taxco

Acapulco

Rio Grande R.

Monterrey

SIERRA MADRE ORIENTAL

CENTRAL PLATEAU

Dolores Hidalgo

Lake Patzcuaro

SIERRA MADRE OCCIDENTAL

BAJA (LOWER) CALIFORNIA

PACIFIC OCEAN

A Land
of Contrasts

Mexico—whose official name is *Los Estados Unidos Mexicanos*, the United States of Mexico—is a land of striking contrasts.

There are, first of all, the contrasts in the land itself, which is larger than California and Alaska together. Long stretches of the eastern coast, along the Gulf of Mexico, are so low and swampy that houses must be built on stilts or heaped-up mounds of earth, to keep them above water. The cattle in these regions stand in water up to their knees, among long-legged water birds, grazing on water hyacinths.

Central Mexico, on the other hand, is a high, arid, cactus-dotted plateau, in many places more than a mile (1.6 km) above sea level. The volcanic mountain ranges that rim its sides are even higher. Some of the peaks of the Sierra Madre Oriental on the east, and the Sierra Madre Occidental on the west, tower more than 3 miles (4.8 km) into the sky.

These differences in altitude bring about the contrasts in Mexico's climate. The country's low-lying coasts are tropical, including its two big peninsulas—Baja (Lower) California along the Pacific and thumb-shaped Yucatán thrusting out into the Gulf of Mexico. Many low inland valleys are also hot, with steamy jungles where orchids grow on every tree and brilliant green parrots flash through the shadows.

But the Central Plateau is cool. And the highest mountain peaks are covered with snow the year around.

Another kind of contrast is this: Mexico has always been a nation of farms, tiny villages, and small towns, with few real cities. But in the past few decades those cities have greatly increased in size. One of them—Mexico City, the nation's capital—is already among the largest on earth. If its growth continues at its present rate, it will have a population of more than thirty million by the year 2,000, and be the largest metropolis in the history of the world.

There are great contrasts, too, among the ways people live. A small number of Mexican landowners and industrialists are enormously rich. In some cases they gained their wealth, at least partly, through the graft and corruption that have always been an accepted part of Mexico's government. A middle class, though now growing steadily, is not nearly as large as the middle class in the United States and most of Europe. And a large proportion of Mexico's population is still—as it has always been—extremely poor.

Wealthy families live in country houses called *haciendas*, or in luxurious city mansions protected by high walls. Middle class families live in comfortable tile-roofed suburban homes or city apartments. Mexico's country poor live in small dirt-floored homes, where they sleep on mats or in hammocks, and cook over an open fire with water carried from the village well. The thousands who crowd into the cities every year, in search of work, can find shelter only in patched-together shacks and shantytowns that often have no sanitation, no electricity, and no safe drinking water.

Independence monument, symbol of Mexico City, on Paseo de la Reforma

Since 1977, when vast new reserves of oil and natural gas were discovered in Mexico, the country's government-owned petroleum industry has boomed. Mexico has become one of the four richest democracies in the Western Hemisphere, along with the United States, Canada, and oil-rich Venezuela. And the government has declared it will use its new oil wealth to carry out, at last, the promises it made many years ago. The promises are to abolish illiteracy and disease and bring prosperity to all its people.

Many Mexicans believe those promises will never be kept, and they give two reasons for their belief. One reason is, they say, that too much of the new wealth will find its way into the pockets of those who have some connection with the government. The other reason is the rapid growth of Mexico's population. No government, these people point out, could provide the millions of new jobs, and the new schools and medical services, which would be needed if all Mexicans were to have the good life the Mexican government has promised.

Therefore, these people say, there will always be a vast contrast between the groups of Mexicans on either side of the country's middle class: those who have great wealth, and who can afford the best education and the finest medical care; and the millions of poor who cannot afford decent homes or decent food, who have little or no education, and who often live and die without ever having seen a doctor.

One more striking contrast in Mexico is the contrast between old and new. It has many forms.

Heavy new trucks, for example, transport Mexican fuel oil over modern highways. Alongside those same highways men, women, and children, and small burros, plod homeward bearing loads of firewood on their backs.

Mexico City has a new 52-acre (20.8-ha) shopping center which is the largest in all Latin America and offers its customers the latest fashions in clothes and all sorts of imported goods from every part of the world. But along the city's sidewalks, barefooted villagers, who have come to the city to sell their wares, pile their sugarcane stalks, their fruits, and nuts on the ground, just as they do at their weekly markets at home.

A single building in the capital represents one of the country's greatest contrasts between old and new. It is the National Museum of Anthropology. Experts from all over the world have said this great stone-and-glass building, completed in 1965, will be the model for many museums of the future. One English visitor said it was a generation ahead of the museums in the United States, and a century ahead of those in England. Yet the Museum's greatest treasures are some of the oldest handmade objects ever found in all of North America—stone and clay figures made by Indians who lived in Mexico thousands of years ago.

Indians in a Museum

Today about thirty out of every hundred Mexicans are pure-blood Indians. They belong to more than fifty Indian groups, each with its own language and customs. A few still speak only their own tongue, and live in the same part of the country their ancestors have inhabited for centuries. Maya (*my*-uh) Indians, for example, still live in the Yucatán peninsula. Zapotec (*zap*-uh-tek) Indians still live in the Oaxaca (wa-*ha*-ka) valley in southern Mexico. Otomi (ohd-uh-*me*) Indians, who are among the poorest in all the country, still live on the arid Central Plateau.

Ten out of every hundred Mexicans are of European stock. Some of these people are descended from the land's Spanish conquerors, who came to Mexico in 1519 and ruled it for three hundred years. Others belong to Spanish families who fled here during Spain's Civil War in the 1930s.

By far the largest group of Mexicans—about sixty out of every hundred—are of part Indian and part European stock. They are called *mestizos*, the Spanish word for "mixed."

The Aztec calendar stone was found beneath the Zócalo, the main square of Mexico City. It had been buried when the Spanish destroyed the Aztec capital, Tenochtitlán. The face at the center of the twenty-five-ton stone is Tonatiuh, the sun god.

Many Mexicans were once almost ashamed of their Indian background. This way of thinking had been inherited from the days of Spanish rule, when the Spaniards looked down on all dark-skinned people and treated the Indians as slaves. But this attitude has been changing since more people have learned about the remarkable Indian civilizations that existed in Mexico long before the Spaniards arrived.

At the National Museum of Anthropology, Mexicans can see models of ancient Indian cities that probably had populations of three hundred thousand or so. Some of those cities were almost certainly larger than the largest European cities of their time. Around their vast paved squares, and along their broad avenues, stood elaborate palaces and templed pyramids. Gardens bloomed with flowers. Orchards produced many kinds of fruit. In huge marketplaces hundreds of varieties of goods were bought and sold— meat and vegetables and grains, pottery and jewelry, and woven cloth and straw.

One disk-shaped carved stone served as a calendar for the Aztecs, the most powerful Indian group in Mexico when the Spaniards arrived. The Aztecs were skilled astronomers and mathematicians. Their calendar, based on a cycle of fifty-two years, was more accurate than any the Europeans had yet developed.

A big stone head just outside the Museum weighs many tons. A giant truck had to be specially designed to bring it to Mexico City from the place near the coast where it was found. The Indians who carved the head centuries ago transported the huge stone from its quarry to their city without the help of any wheeled vehicle at all. They used wheels only on toys.

Every day the Museum is visited by foreigners from many lands, and by busloads of children brought here from their schools in every part of Mexico. The Museum was built by the Mexican government as part of its education program. Every day it helps people understand Mexico's ancient Indian heritage.

The Early People

The earliest inhabitants of Mexico left no written records that can be read today. Therefore their full story will probably never be known. But thousands of things they made and used have been found, and more are being found every year. They help archeologists and anthropologists piece together at least a sketchy story of Mexico's early Indian past.

Many scientists now believe nomadic hunters were wandering through Mexico as many as thirty thousand years ago. Perhaps these early people came from Asia by way of the land that once connected Asia to Alaska. Perhaps some came from Africa.

As time went by and certain nomadic people learned to sow and harvest crops, they settled in tribal villages. The people of each tribe developed their own culture, or way of life, suited to the particular place where they lived.

Tribes living in the Central Plateau, for example, built homes of sun-dried clay, or adobe, and roofed them with thick layers of grass. They made fences of cactus. Homes in tropical regions were made of slender saplings or canes, tied together and roofed with palm leaves. The same kind of homes are still practical in Mexico

today. An adobe house keeps out the hot noon sun and holds in the warmth of the fire at night. Cane-walled houses are airy even on the hottest days.

Each early Indian tribe had its own gods. In dry regions the Indians prayed to a god of rain and carried out elaborate ceremonies to win his favor. People also worshiped gods of the sun and the moon and goddesses of corn. They made stone or clay images of these gods, some large, others small enough to keep in their homes. They built temples in their honor.

A temple usually stood on a flat-topped pyramid made of rubble and faced with stone and plaster. Sometimes the slanting sides of the pyramid were smooth. Sometimes they rose upward in huge steps or terraces. The outer stone was often decorated with carved and painted designs. Steep flights of stairs led to the top.

Some Indian tribes enlarged or rebuilt their pyramids from time to time. They heaped rubble over the whole structure and then gave it a new facing of stone. A pyramid thus became a series of pyramids, one inside the other, separated by layers of rubble.

Around their templed pyramids Indians built palaces for their chiefs or rulers and for the priests who led their religious ceremonies. Often they also built a huge stone-walled field or court where they played a game with a hard rubber ball. Today no one knows the rules of their game. Probably the players tried to throw the ball through one of the two stone circles fastened to the walls of the court.

All the ancient cities of Mexico grew up around these groups of buildings, and probably each city was the center of a number of small farming villages. The various cities traded with each other and fought each other. Sometimes they adopted each other's ideas

The Maya temple of Kukulcan at Chichén Itzá rises from Yucatán's flat plain. The pyramid has 365 steps, the number of days in the civil year; the terraces are divided into the number of years in the sacred calendar.

and ways of life. The culture of the most advanced people usually spread to people who were less advanced.

About 450 B.C., the Olmec culture influenced people in many parts of Mexico and what is now Central America. Very little is known about these mysterious people. The Olmec were apparently the first to carve big stone monuments, such as the great head at the National Museum of Anthropology.

Other peoples reached the peak of their culture and influence during the next period, from about 200 B.C. to A.D. 850. Two of the most famous were the Maya and the Zapotec, both builders of magnificent cities. A third was the group of people who built what is now the most famous ruined city in Mexico, the city of Teotihuacán (tay-o-tee-wa-*kan*), thirty miles (48 km) from Mexico City.

The name of the builders of Teotihuacán is unknown. Even the original name of the city is lost. Its present name was given to it by the Aztecs, who saw the city only after it had lain in ruins for five hundred years. But even then it seemed so magnificent that the Aztecs thought it must have been built by gods or giants. The name they gave it means "the place where those who die turn into gods."

Archeologists have been exploring Teotihuacán for years. They know that its broad avenues and plazas were paved with many layers of smooth plaster and that the walls of many buildings were covered with brilliant paintings. They believe that it was the largest city in the Western world before the days of the Spanish conquest. It spread over twenty-five square miles (65 sq. km) of the broad valley of Mexico, in the middle of the Central Plateau.

The biggest pyramid in Teotihuacán, now called the Pyramid of the Sun, is seven hundred feet (210 m) square and over two hundred feet (60 m) high. Near it is the Pyramid of the Moon (about one hundred and fifty feet (45 m) high) and a temple to the god

Quetzalcóatl, god of life and learning,
is sculpted as a plumed serpent on the
walls of the temple to him at Teotihuacán.

Quetzalcóatl (kayt-sahl-*koh*'atl), sometimes called the Plumed Serpent. Another smaller building has been named the Butterfly Palace, because many of its carved decorations are in the form of butterflies.

About the year 900, Teotihuacán and other great centers of culture were destroyed by warlike tribes from the north. These wandering invaders, the Chichimec (chee-chee-*mayk*), brought an end to what archeologists call the greatest period of Mexican Indian civilization.

For a time one group of Chichimec, the Toltec, settled in cities that they built themselves or took from others. They took over Cholula (cho-*loo*-la), southeast of Mexico City, which had many large temples and palaces. The Toltec filled all these buildings and the open spaces around them with adobe bricks. Then they buried everything under one great heap of rubble. They had transformed the whole center of the city into one huge pyramid, or altar platform.

Later the slopes of that great pyramid were overgrown with trees and plants. Today it looks like a natural hill. The building on top of it now is a Christian church.

Eventually the Toltec, too, were destroyed by new waves of Chichimec. One of the last of the invading Chichimec groups was the Aztecs, or Mexica, the people who gave their name to the modern nation of Mexico.

The Aztecs

The Aztecs came into the Central Plateau seeking a place to live. A legend says that they asked their gods where they should settle, and the gods gave them a sign to look for—an eagle with a snake in its mouth, perched on a cactus. The eagle appeared to them on an island in the big shallow lake then covering part of the valley of Mexico. On that island the Aztecs founded their city of Tenochtitlán (tay-noch-tee-*tlan*) in 1325.

During the next two centuries the Aztecs grew rich and strong. They conquered other tribes and forced them to pay tribute every year. Together with two other cities on the shore of the lake, they formed a confederation that finally controlled over half of present-day Mexico.

In the outlying farming regions around an Aztec city, each man cultivated the plot of ground assigned to him when he married. The plot did not belong to him, but to his tribe. He also worked in the fields that supplied food for the tribe's priests and other leaders. Men cultivated the fields together, just as many Mexicans work on cooperative farms today.

*Mexicans and visitors enjoy the floating
gardens of Xochimilco. In the foreground
are dug-out canoes called* chinampas.

When the island city of Tenochtitlán needed more land, the Aztecs created other "islands" in the lake. They built frameworks of twigs and woven reeds and filled them with earth and planted seeds. For a time the frameworks floated about. Then plant roots took hold on the lake bottom, and the islands were anchored fast. Men traveled among them in swift canoes.

Some of those "floating islands" still exist at a place called Xochimilco (so-chee-*meel*-ko), on the outskirts of Mexico City. Farmers go to them each day by boat to tend their crops of flowers and vegetables. On sunny Sundays thousands of visitors ride among the islands in boats decorated with flowers. The owner of each boat usually spells out the name of his sweetheart in the flowery arch rising at the front of the craft.

The Aztecs raised corn and squash and gourds, chile peppers, alligator pears, and tomatoes. They grew the tobacco that they smoked in long hollow reeds, and the cotton that the Aztec women wove into cloth. They planted big fields of the spiny-leaved cactus called *agave*, and used it in all the ways that it is still used in Mexico today. They made a drink from its sap, and rope and a coarse cloth from its fiber. They used its thorns as needles, and thatched their roofs with its big flat spiny leaves.

An Aztec farmer spent his spare time chipping out stone knives and weapons, making pottery bowls, weaving baskets and mats, and making ornaments of feathers, gold, and precious stones. He took some of these things to the big city market, and exchanged them for things that he was not able to make himself. If he wanted to trade a bowl for some more valuable object, such as a knife, he made up the difference with cocoa beans. Cocoa, or chocolate, was a favorite drink of the Aztecs. The word "chocolate" comes from their language.

The Aztecs became skillful engineers. When they found that the water in the lake was not good for drinking, they built an aqueduct that brought fresh water to their city from a hill several miles away. They also built causeways that connected Tenochtitlán with friendly cities on the shore. Drawbridges in the causeways could be pulled up if an enemy approached.

In 1502, Moctezuma (mok-ta-*zoo*-ma) II or Montezuma became chief of the Aztecs. He had three thousand servants and lived in a magnificent palace of one hundred rooms. His royal cloak was made of feathers from the tropical birds caged in the royal zoo. His highly organized army often marched out to war and brought back prisoners to serve as slaves or to be sacrificed to the Aztec war god. Moctezuma was the richest and most powerful chief in all Mexico.

Moctezuma and Cortés

In 1519, Moctezuma heard that white-skinned strangers had landed on the Mexican coast.

These white men were soldiers and priests led by the daring young Spanish captain Hernán Cortés. Cortés hoped to win wealth and glory by conquering Mexico for his king and converting the native Indians to Christianity. He felt certain that he would succeed. He had already seen the primitive little Indian villages on the islands of Cuba and Hispaniola, and expected to find the same kind of settlements in Mexico.

But his scouts soon told him of big Indian cities near the coast and of Moctezuma's great capital and powerful army.

Cortés had only a few hundred soldiers, and some wanted to sail away as soon as they heard the news. Then a messenger from Moctezuma arrived and said that the Aztec chief welcomed the white men to the coast of Mexico, but warned them not to go inland. Moctezuma had also sent gifts to Cortés, including gold ornaments and a helmet filled with grains of gold.

When Cortés saw the gold, he decided that Mexico was a rich land worth fighting for. To prevent his soldiers from deserting him, he burned his ships. Then he ordered his little army to follow him westward toward Tenochtitlán.

It was a long journey through jungles and over mountains. The Spaniards gained some allies on the way among tribes who hated or feared the Aztecs. The chiefs of these tribes gave them food and armies of warriors. They even offered the white men their daughters in marriage.

The invaders also met Indians loyal to Moctezuma, who tried to drive them back. The Spaniards' guns and horses saved them. The Indians had never seen either of these things before. The noisy booms of the guns frightened them. They thought a man on horseback must be a god with a human head and body and the legs of an animal. So the Indians often surrendered even when they far outnumbered the enemy.

Finally Cortés reached Tenochtitlán, and there a strange thing happened. Moctezuma came to greet him and invited him to enter the city as his guest.

The reason for Moctezuma's invitation still puzzles historians today. Some say that Moctezuma believed Cortés was an ancient Indian god who had disappeared long before and was now returning to rule the Aztecs.

For many days Cortés and his men were entertained in a large palace. Some of the soldiers were so dazzled by the wealth and luxury around them that they thought they must be dreaming. Then trouble occurred.

The Spaniards killed Aztec priests and destroyed images of Aztec gods. Moctezuma's subjects grew angry and wanted to destroy the white men. Cortés tricked Moctezuma into joining him

These drawings of the conquest of Tenochtitlán are from the Codex Florentino, *a picture book by Aztec scribes. Mounted on horses, Cortés and his men approach the city (top) and then follow the causeway in, to be met by Aztec warriors.*

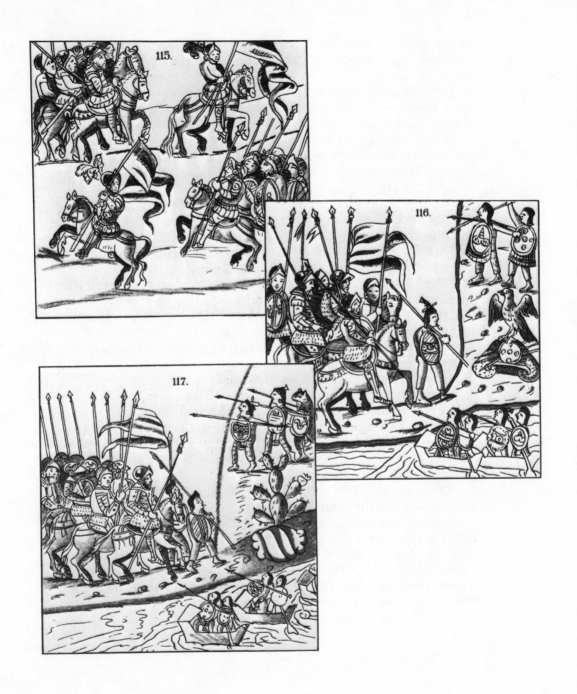

at his headquarters, and threatened to kill him if the Aztecs attacked. But fighting did break out. Moctezuma was slain by a stone thrown by his own people when he tried to convince them to stop the attack. The Spaniards were forced to flee, swimming for their lives toward the shore of the lake. Some were so heavily weighted with stolen gold that they sank and drowned.

But Cortés did not leave Mexico. He gathered new allies among the Aztecs' enemies, the Tlaxcaltecas (tlas-*kal*-te-kas), and built ships that would permit him to attack by water. Early in 1521, he returned to lay siege to the Aztecs' island city.

The defenders of Tenochtitlán, under Moctezuma's nephew Cuauhtémoc (kwow-*tay*-mok), fought fiercely. But after three months their city fell. The Spaniards tortured Cuauhtémoc to make him reveal the location of the Aztec treasure, which he insisted had been thrown in the lake. Later they killed him.

The Spanish *conquistadores*, or conquerors, forced the Indians to destroy their own city and build a new one for the victors in its place. The stones of the great pyramid were taken apart, one by one, and used to build a Christian cathedral. Moctezuma's palace was torn down and a new palace for Cortés was built where it had stood. Both buildings faced a huge plaza, or square, which today is the most historic spot in Mexico.

Mexico's Spanish past is still alive in that square, which is now the center of modern Mexico's capital. Mexicans call that square the Zócalo. Its official name is *La Plaza de la Constitución*, or Constitution Plaza. The Spanish-built cathedral still stands. The president of Mexico sits in a palace the Spaniards built after Cortés's palace was destroyed in 1692.

Of course no Aztec buildings are left standing for modern Mexicans to see. But they can watch the archeologists who are carefully uncovering the Aztec ruins on which Cortés built this big square. Other sights nearby are reminders of the Aztecs too: the many buildings that are slowly sinking, year by year, into the spongy soil beneath them. That soil is spongy because Mexico City stands on those "floating islands" the Aztecs created in the shallow lake where they founded their own city of Tenochtitlán.

New Spain

Under Cortés, and the Spanish rulers who followed him, Mexico was governed as a colony of Spain, known as New Spain. It extended far north into what is now the United States, including most of New Mexico, Arizona, California, and Texas.

The Spaniards who came to settle there gave the land its official language, its money—based on a coin called a *peso*—and its beast of burden, the patient burro. They founded new cities with Spanish names such as Veracruz (veer-uh-*crooz*) and San Antonio. They also added the names of Christian saints to those of the Mexican towns. A place called Topiltopec, for example, became San Pedro Topiltopec. Priests baptized its inhabitants and told them that they were now Christians and that Saint Peter would guard them as their patron saint.

The Spaniards' homes and palaces were built in the style that they had known in Europe. Rooms opened off central courtyards. Floors and roofs were tiled. Iron grillwork protected windows overlooking the street.

On the vast tracts of land granted to them by their king, the Spaniards carried out large-scale mining, started industries to supply their own needs, and introduced new crops and new kinds of domestic animals.

Cortés, for example, received large grants of land in and around the city of Mexico and in the beautiful valley of Oaxaca farther south. He opened gold and silver mines which earned him a fortune, even though the Spanish throne claimed one-fifth of all the colony's mineral wealth. He started sugarcane plantations with plants brought in from Cuba, and built sugar mills. He imported sheep and other kinds of cattle. He planted groves of mulberry trees to feed the silkworms that he introduced.

Indians did all the labor on Cortés's fields and in his mines. They were the same people who had once owned the land that was now his. There were over twenty-three thousand of them, the inhabitants of more than twenty towns and villages. Now they were all landless and forbidden by law to grow or to make anything for their own profit. They had to work from dawn to dusk for barely enough food to keep them alive. Many died in the dangerous mines. Others died of the diseases that the white men had brought—measles, smallpox, and tuberculosis.

In all Mexico only a few tribes had managed to escape into the mountains where the Spaniards could not find them. The rest were forced to slave for the white conquerors.

The king of Spain had granted the Catholic church thousands of acres of land for the support of Indian schools. Many priests began to learn Indian languages so that they could talk to their pupils without an interpreter. But the landowners thought that Indian children did not need to know anything except the few skills that would make them useful in the fields, in the mines, or as servants in the big homes. Priests, afraid to act against the landowners' wishes, built only a few Indian schools. The church, too, grew rich on its vast properties.

Most Spaniards thought that the Indians were being treated as well as they deserved. "They were warlike heathen," the conquerors said. "We have brought them peace. And we have saved their souls by converting them to Christianity."

It was true that the various tribes no longer had the opportunity or weapons for battle. But the presence of the Spaniards had not united them all into a single people. And their conversion to Christianity was not complete. Many Indians felt that a white-skinned Jesus Christ and Virgin Mary had nothing to do with them. They still worshiped their own gods in secret. Those who did become true Christians gave their devotion to the Virgin of Guadalupe, the Indians' own saint. Her story is told every year on December 12, when thousands of people make pilgrimages to her shrine. Our Lady of Guadalupe is now the patron saint of Mexico.

The story says that one day in 1531, Juan Diego, a poor Indian boy, climbed a hill at a place called Guadalupe (*gwad*-ul-oop) near Mexico City. Suddenly there appeared on the path before him a beautiful dark-skinned lady in a blue cloak. She told him that the Virgin Mary had come to look after his people, and that the bishop should build a church in her honor on the spot where she stood.

Juan hurried to the bishop's palace with his tale. The bishop refused to believe that a saint would appear to a poor Indian, or that a saint could have a dark skin. He sent Juan away.

Juan returned to the hill and again the lady appeared. He confessed that he had failed to carry out her wish. She smiled at him, and at that moment roses sprang out of the barren soil at her feet. She told Juan to take the flowers to the bishop as proof of his story. Juan gathered the roses, wrapped them in his shabby cape, and carried them to the city. When he opened the cape in front of the bishop, a portrait of the lady had miraculously appeared on the cloth.

Then the bishop believed in Juan's vision, and in honor of the Virgin he ordered a church to be built on the hill at Guadalupe. Almost three hundred years later, when the Indians finally rose up against Spain, they fought under the Virgin's banner. Their first leader in that struggle was Father Miguel Hidalgo (ee-*dahl*-go), who sounded the call to arms now repeated each year to open the celebration of Mexico's Independence Day, September 16.

Fight for Freedom

Father Hidalgo (1753–1811) was one of many Spanish priests who tried to help the Indians. He believed in the democratic ideals of the revolutions then taking place in the American colonies and in France. He wanted the Indians to become independent of their masters.

The landowners and church authorities, who thought Father Hidalgo was a dangerous man, tried to get rid of him. But he had friends among the growing number of ambitious young Spaniards who wanted independence for the colony of New Spain. He agreed to raise an army of Indians to help those Spaniards fight for freedom. He believed that freedom for Mexico would mean that the land taken away from the Indians would be restored to them.

On September 16, 1810, Father Hidalgo rang the bell of his parish church in Dolores (now Dolores Hidalgo in his honor), to call out the men of the neighborhood. Thousands of Indians eventually joined in the revolution that began that day. So did thousands of mestizos who had been badly treated by the Spaniards. Fighting side by side, they all began, for the first time, to have a feeling of unity.

The Revolution was not won easily. It dragged on for years. Sometimes it died down into an uneasy peace and then flared up again.

Another priest, José María Morelos (1765–1815), led the rebels after Father Hidalgo was killed in 1811. His army, too, was defeated, and Morelos was shot by a Spanish firing squad. Then Vincente Guerrero (gay-*ray*-roh) (1783–1831), an Indian, carried on the battle almost alone for a time. Finally he was joined by the forces of Augustín de Iturbide (ee-toor-*bee*-day) (1783–1824), a Spanish army officer who had turned against Spain. Together, in 1821, they defeated the royal forces and established Mexico's independence.

Iturbide promptly declared himself emperor of Mexico. Landowners and church officials rejoiced. They had been afraid that they would lose all their wealth and power if Mexico became a republic, as Guerrero's rebels had planned. So these rebels had to fight once more to force Iturbide into exile and give themselves the chance to elect their first president. In 1824, they chose one of their own generals, a man who called himself Guadalupe Victoria, in honor of the rebels' banner. His name meant "The Virgin of Guadalupe triumphant!"

The weak young republic soon faced a serious threat from outside. Colonists from the eastern United States who had settled in northern Mexico declared their region to be a separate nation called Texas. The Mexican government sent forces to bring them back into the republic. Eventually, in 1846, the United States got into the war. It invaded and defeated Mexico, which was forced to sign away more than half its territory to the victorious Americans in 1848. Mexico lost all its land north of the river they call the Rio Bravo. North Americans call it the Rio Grande.

After that tragic war, Benito Juárez (*hwa*-rez) (1806–1872), a Zapotec Indian, became the leader of his shrunken nation. When he took the president's chair in 1861, everyone knew what his program would be. He was determined that his people should regain possession of their own land long occupied by the Spaniards. Church authorities and big landowners, those old enemies of the people, asked Napoleon III to help them keep their property.

Napoleon had become emperor after France had been a republic for a time. He thought that his own position would be strengthened if he could transform the republic of Mexico into an empire too. So he sent an army to Mexico, along with the Austrian archduke, Maximilian. Maximilian was crowned Emperor of Mexico in 1864, while French soldiers drove Juárez out of the capital and guarded the property that he had threatened.

Maximilian and his beautiful wife Carlota had been told that the whole country would welcome them. Instead, they found themselves hated by most of the people. When the French forces left at the end of three years, the unhappy emperor's friends could not protect him. Carlota sailed for France to plead for help, but it was too late. Maximilian's empire collapsed; he was shot by the followers of Juárez, in 1867, and Juárez himself returned in triumph.

Mexico had finally won its political independence. Its people were determined never again to be ruled by another power.

Father Hidalgo rang the bell of this parish church in Dolores to signal the beginning of the revolution.

Fight
for Land

From 1867 until his death five years later, Juárez struggled to give his people justice under a constitution patterned on that of the United States. He made little progress. One of his strongest former supporters, Porfirio Díaz (1830–1915), had become his enemy because Díaz also wanted to be president. Twice Díaz raised an army against the government, and in 1876 he succeeded in seizing power. He ruled as a dictator for thirty-four years.

Díaz insisted that he wanted to make Mexico prosperous. Many said he succeeded. But the new wealth which he helped to create was all in the hands of a small group of men, including many from the United States and other countries. Some of these foreigners made millions of dollars from land and people they never even saw. Mexican workers on their land were paid almost nothing. The land was drained of valuable natural resources—oil, timber, and minerals.

When the desperate and landless poor rose up once again, their leader was Francisco Madero (1873–1913), a wealthy landowner's son who believed in democracy. Díaz had thrown Madero in jail for daring to run against him for the presidency. Madero had escaped and raised the army that fought Mexico's important Revolution of 1910—a revolution for agrarian, or land, reform.

Emiliano Zapata (sa-*pa*-ta) (1877–1919), often called Mexico's Robin Hood, led one of the ragged bands of fighters. Pancho Villa (*vee*-uh) (1877–1923), a picturesque bandit, led another. Factory workers, miners, and railroad workers joined the revolt too.

The new wave of revolutionists ruthlessly burned churches and tore the robes from priests who had supported the landowners. They burned hundreds of big ranchers' homes, slaughtered the owners, and gave the dead men's land to the workers who had slaved on it.

Chaos followed the revolution's victory in 1911. Presidents came and went. One held office for less than an hour. The stability of modern Mexico, most people agree, did not really begin until Lázaro Cárdenas (*car*-de-nas) (1895–1970) became president in 1934.

Cárdenas was the first president to make real use of the land-distribution laws that had been written into Mexico's constitution. Those laws stated that no person might own more than 250 acres (100 ha) of good farmland, and that the government should break up the country's huge ranches and distribute those thousands of acres among the people who worked on them.

Cárdenas not only broke up many large old Mexican-owned ranches; he also took over large properties owned by foreigners. He was thus able to distribute 45 million acres (18 million ha) of land among some million landless families. Many of the new landowners formed government-sponsored cooperatives, called *ejidos* (e-*hee*-dos), and farmed their land together. Ejidos could buy equipment a single small landowner couldn't afford.

Cárdenas had made a good beginning, people said, toward turning Father Hidalgo's dream into reality. It seemed possible that in the near future every person who wanted his own land would actually have it.

Since Cárdenas left office in 1940, some three million more

Mexicans have been given land. But the number of landless families increases as the population grows, and today there are at least another three million hoping for land of their own.

One reason those people are still without land is that there are still many large properties in Mexico. The wealthy owners of those big holdings have used political influence, and paid bribes, to prevent their land from being broken up. Even when a large farm has been officially divided into small plots, and those plots have been assigned to waiting families, the owner is often able to delay the actual distribution from year to year. And when families have sometimes taken over the land promised to them, they have been thrown off by the landowner's hired guards, or by the local police or soldiers supplied by the Mexican army.

Some of the large farms in Mexico today have been put together since Cárdenas's day, out of many 250-acre (100-ha) plots. Since each Mexican—even a small baby—is allowed to own that much land, large families have been able to acquire thousands of acres.

Experts point out, however, that even if all the large farms were broken up, there would simply not be enough arable land to provide farms for all the families still waiting for them. And the experts explain why: of Mexico's nearly 490 million acres (196 million ha), only 60 million acres (24 million ha) are good farm land; and only another 8 million acres (3.2 million ha), they say, could be "made" out of land that is naturally too mountainous, or too swampy, or too dry for farming.

The government has already been "making" more good land. By building dams and irrigation projects in the Pacific coastal regions, for example, it has transformed thousands of dry acres there into valuable crop land. It is also persuading families to move into the tropical jungles of Yucatán, to clear and plant land that has never before been cultivated—although some farming experts believe the thin layer of top soil there cannot support yearly harvests.

There are certain farming experts and economists in Mexico today who say that efforts to continue the land-distribution program should be halted. The reason is that most farmers who now own small plots are not able to afford good seeds, fertilizers, or proper equipment. Their crops are therefore so meager that they can't support their families. A typical small farmer, for example, grows only about one-fifth as much corn per acre of his land as an Illinois farmer does. Even those who belong to cooperatives are in many cases no better off. Their commonly-held land may be worn out, or lack enough water, or be badly managed by ill-trained or corrupt ejido directors.

Only large efficiently managed farms, these experts say, can make the necessary investment in seeds, fertilizers, and labor-saving machinery. Although they realize that such farms throw thousands of Mexicans out of work, they believe the government should encourage them. Only this kind of farming, they say, can improve agricultural production.

Many government officials who agree with them don't say so openly. They are afraid of angering Mexicans long devoted to the idea of land for all—the idea for which the 1910 revolution was fought and won. But those officials hope—and many other Mexicans do, too—that the idea may some day belong to Mexico's past: a proud part of its history, but no longer a goal for its future.

Farms and Farming

There is almost nothing that will not grow in one part of Mexico or another. Corn can be raised almost everywhere. Wheat, strawberries, and a variety of orchard fruits and vegetables thrive in the cool uplands, along with fields of cotton. Coffee, Mexico's most valuable export crop, grows in the warmer regions, where limes and oranges, bananas and coconuts, and papayas and other tropical fruits flourish. A good deal of land that is too poor for crops of any kind can support sheep or cattle.

Corn, the basis of Mexico's diet, was for centuries the country's largest crop and long one of its important exports. But in the early 1970s Mexico found it was no longer producing even enough corn to feed its own people. In 1973 it had to start importing corn, chiefly from the United States. One reason for this, of course, was the country's rapidly growing population. Another reason was that much of the best land had been given over to fruits and vegetables which could be exported for high prices. Growers had learned that an acre planted to cherry tomatoes, for example, earned four times as much money as an acre planted to corn.

Most of the fruits and vegetables Mexico produces for export today are raised by a few hundred growers in northwestern Mexico, on mechanized farms covering thousands of acres. Those farms, described by some Mexicans as "the backyard of the United States," use American-made tractors, American-made pesticides, and often American seed, to grow crops that only Americans can afford to buy. Those crops, Mexicans also point out, are often canned or frozen or dried in plants owned by multinational companies—that is, companies which conduct business in many parts of the world. And those companies, they say, are controlled by Americans.

Many of Mexico's poor, therefore, feel the United States is partly responsible for their poverty. Resentment against their big neighbor to the north is not a new feeling for them. They still remember that in 1848 the United States defeated their armies and "stole" all Mexican territory north of the Rio Grande.

Most poor Mexican farmers, however, feel their own government is also to blame for their poverty. They accuse it of distributing its agricultural aid unfairly. Seventy percent of that aid goes to the handful of big growers who export fruits and vegetables, to help them irrigate their land, improve their soil, and increase their crops. The thirty percent that is left gives the same kind of help to small farmers and members of ejidos, but it must be spread among thousands of them. They say it is not enough.

One solution to Mexico's corn shortage could be to force the big fruit-and-vegetable growers to raise corn instead, on their fertile, well-watered fields. This could mean that little or no corn would have to be imported from the United States, and many Mexicans think their country should not be dependent on another country for its basic food.

Others say Mexico should go on using its best farming land for crops that can earn large profits in the United States—profits which can pay for efficiently produced American corn.

No one knows how this debate will end. While it goes on, the government plans to use some of its oil profits to give more help to small farmers, so their families can live better. It will also encour-

*This freshwater fish farm near Mexico City is
a government project to increase food production.*

age all the farmers in a neighborhood to operate their plots as one unit, with each farmer sharing in the costs and the profits. It will give more aid to the old ejidos, too. Government farming experts believe these plans should result in more and cheaper food for the whole country.

Another plan for which the government has high hopes is to build food processing plants out in the countryside, in regions where there are many small farms. Such plants could freeze, can, or dry Mexican farm products right where they are grown. This would be more efficient and more profitable than shipping the fresh produce to the cities.

Such plants could also give employment to many landless Mexicans. And, if workers in those plants are paid fair wages, they might decide that they were better off than if they had their own small plots of land. They might then join the many Mexicans who already feel that the idea of land for all has been replaced by an idea that is better for Mexico's growing population: work for all, in decent conditions and at fair wages.

The Bread of Mexico

The reason corn is so important to Mexicans is that corn flour is used to make the flat round *tortilla* (tor-*tee*-ya) that is the bread of the country.

Machine-made tortillas are now sold fresh or frozen in city supermarkets and in stores or markets in smaller towns. But many village women still make their own. The process takes time and skill.

A tortilla-maker first boils dried corn kernels in limewater to soften their tough outer skins and transform them into a pulpy mass called *nixtamal.* Then, if she can afford it, she may take her nixtamal to a village shop or mill to be ground by machine. Or she may grind it herself between two stones. Many people say that the corn should be ground by hand so that it will have what they call "the taste of the stone."

A tortilla-maker often works on her knees. In front of her stands her *metate* (meh-*tah*-tay), the larger of her two stones. It looks like a miniature table with a slanting top and three stubby legs. The smaller stone is a cylinder-shaped roller called a *mano.*

*A Mexican housewife makes
tortillas in the traditional way.*

She rolls the dough between the stones until it has just the right "feel." Then she breaks off a bit of it and flattens it into a circle between her palms. She slaps the circle back and forth, from hand to hand, until it is almost as thin as paper. Then she bakes it on a tin sheet laid over the fire.

A housewife may make a hundred or more of these corn cakes each morning, and another batch later in the day. A man can eat two dozen for his midday meal. The family dog may eat ten.

Tortilla dough is also used to make other things, such as *tamales* and *pozole* (po-*so*-lay). Pozole is a kind of cornmeal mush flavored with meat, vegetables, and spices. A tamale is a handful of moist dough stuffed with bits of meat or chicken and boiled in a wrapping of corn husks.

Finished tortillas are used to make other dishes, too. *Enchiladas*, for example, are made by wrapping tortillas around spiced meat and cooking them in a spicy onion-and-tomato sauce. Tortillas folded over a filling of spiced meat or chicken and then fried crisp are called *tacos*. Hot tacos are sold at roadside and street-corner stands, and at baseball games. People eat them with their fingers.

Plain tortillas appear on most Mexican tables three times a day, for breakfast, dinner, and supper. Even with a big meal of soup, meat, vegetables, salad, and dessert, people usually want several tortillas. Many poor people have nothing for dinner except a handful of *frijoles* (free-*ho*-less), or beans, and tortillas flavored with hot chile pepper.

There is good nourishment in a meal of beans, corn, and chile pepper. But children, especially, need other foods, such as eggs, meat, and wheat flour. White bread made of wheat flour, for example, is now advertised on highway billboards and over radio and television. Huge factories turn out thousands of wrapped loaves a day. Trucks deliver them to stores all over the country. This mass-produced white bread is cheaper than the crusty white rolls that have been popular among the well-to-do ever since the Spaniards came. Many poor people who never bought white rolls, except on holidays, can afford to buy this bread. Some say it will eventually take the place of tortillas.

Others laugh at such an idea. They say a piece of bread is not half as satisfying as a tortilla. Some even say, "Man is meant to live on corn, just as the legend tells us."

Mexico's corn legend says that when the gods first wanted to bring human beings into the world, they decided that they should not do so until they had prepared a food fit for them to eat. The great god Quetzalcóatl took on the task. He transformed himself into an ant and stole a precious kernel of corn. The grain it produced was excellent. And so the gods created people, and they have been nourished by corn ever since.

The Oil Boom

Mexico has been producing oil since the early years of this century. At that time all its wells, drilling rigs, pipelines, and refineries were owned and operated by foreign corporations, most of them United States oil companies. Some Mexicans grew rich through their connections with the foreigners, but the companies took most of their profits out of the country. And their profits were large, because they paid very low wages to the nearly twenty thousand Mexicans they hired as unskilled laborers.

In 1938 President Cárdenas, who had seized foreign-owned farms when he started the land-distribution program, seized the foreign-owned oil wells. He turned them all over to a new company owned by the Mexican government. That company, *Petróleos Mexicanos,* is now known throughout Mexico and the world by its abbreviated name, Pemex.

Pemex faced many difficulties in its first years. It had to repay the foreign companies for their property, and replace the drilling rigs and other equipment those companies had taken out of the country when they left. Since the companies had also taken away their skilled technicians, Pemex had to build up its own staff of geologists and engineers, many of them trained in the United States.

But Pemex managed to keep its wells flowing and its refineries operating. By 1962, when its debt to the foreign companies was paid off, it was producing almost enough petroleum to supply Mexico's needs.

Ten years later, when the country was in a serious economic slump, geologists sought for and began to find new oil fields. By 1979 they had discovered what is now recognized as the fifth largest reserves of oil and natural gas in the world. (Larger oil reserves exist in Saudi Arabia, Kuwait, the Soviet Union, and Iran.) Mexico's reserves could supply far more oil and gas than the country could use. Some of those new-found resources could thus be exported. Energy-hungry nations, including the United States, immediately looked at Mexico with new respect. All hoped to become its customers.

Many Mexicans are proud of the new importance their country has won as a result of its sudden oil boom. Others complain that it has brought nothing but suffering to millions of Mexicans.

New roads and pipelines cut deep gouges across farms in the oil regions, causing low-lying land to flood and ruining fields of sugarcane, beans, and corn. Gases from oil wells have ruined other crops. In some places farmers put up barricades to keep oil workers out. The barricades were always removed and the oil workers moved in. Thousands of farmers have left land they say has been destroyed, and made their way to the cities to crowd into already overcrowded slums.

Pollution has harmed the air and water in the region of the huge new refineries. One refinery near the Gulf of Mexico dumps thousands of gallons of chemicals and poisonous heavy metals every day into the Coatzacoalcos River. Petrochemical plants nearby dump their wastes into the streams that feed the Coatzacoalcos. Women in villages along its banks must push aside the scum of heavy oil on the river's surface, before they can dip up water for drinking and cooking. The river's crabs and fish, which once provided a living for village fishermen, are polluted and unsafe to eat.

A dark layer of smoke hides the sky, making people cough and giving them severe headaches. They say that many of them will probably have to die before anything is done to control the region's pollution.

But Pemex, now the nation's largest employer, gives jobs to 100,000 workers. Only fifteen percent of all Mexican workers belong to a union, but all the Pemex workers do, and they earn good wages. Pemex profits provide almost three-quarters of the government's budget.

The government has pledged to export its oil and gas at a slow, steady pace. This will make the reserves last as long as possible, and give Mexico time to establish new sources of income that will support the country when the oil and gas are gone. Also, government experts say, they don't want money flowing into the country faster than it can be wisely spent.

Its plans for spending its new money are already well known. It is oil money that Mexico hopes will rebuild its troubled agriculture, provide jobs for the unemployed, and pay for the new programs of education, medical care, transportation, and housing that Mexico has needed for so long.

Refineries, such as this Pemex
complex at Minatitlán, are a
vital part of the Mexican economy.

Made in Mexico

Mexico was an agricultural country when World War II began in 1939. The manufactured goods it had to import from the United States and other industrial nations were paid for by exports of grain and valuable raw materials.

The war changed that situation abruptly. Industrial nations, busy supplying their armed forces, no longer sent Mexico what it needed. When mining equipment, cars, and other goods wore out, they could not be replaced. Breakdowns occurred in basic public services. The government decided to prevent another such disaster in the future. After the war it invited foreign manufacturers to help it introduce a program of industrialization in Mexico. Many companies accepted because they believed Mexican investments would be profitable.

Those foreign companies built factories in Mexican cities and imported and installed the equipment they needed. They also brought in engineers, chemists, and plant managers to run them, and to train Mexicans to take their places some day.

The program caused some problems. Thousands of poor people, leaving the countryside in the hope of finding factory jobs, started the city-bound movement that still troubles Mexico today. Mexico's dependence on the United States increased, because so much of the foreign investment came from there.

But the program did succeed. Today the words, *Hecho en Mexico*—Made in Mexico—are stamped on almost all the manufactured goods Mexicans buy. Today Mexico can also export manufactured goods. And it hopes to export much more of them in the future. Economists say it must do so, because more industries—and more exports—offer the best way to supply enough jobs for Mexico's workers.

Half of Mexico's work force is now unable to earn a decent living, and every year that work force is increased by about a million new job seekers. So the Mexican government is urging its industrialists to expand their factories or build new ones—in partnership, if necessary, with foreign companies. To persuade industrialists to build new plants in the countryside, away from the cities, the government offers low tax rates, and cheap electricity, gas, oil, and transportation to those who do so. The Mexican government can make such an offer because, along with Pemex and the country's telephone and telegraph system, it owns the light and power industry, and the railroads and airline.

Not all things made in Mexico are made in its factories, of course. In villages all over the country, craftsmen and craftswomen make the same woven baskets, handwoven cloth, clay pots, and other things that their Indian ancestors made centuries ago. Some still take their products to village markets each week. But in those markets they must compete, often unsuccessfully, with sellers of plastic baskets, machine-woven cloth, and aluminum pots. Many craftsmen and craftswomen have therefore found another way to sell their wares, with the help of government experts.

"If Mexican women are buying fewer clay pots," those experts tell them, "tourists are buying more. Tourists are interested in all the handmade things you can turn out right here in your own village."

*Young craftswomen still use
back-strap looms to weave
beautifully patterned fabrics.*

Oaxacan black pottery, made by starving
the kiln of oxygen during the firing.
In the background, potters mold the clay.

Some of Mexico's finest handcrafted articles may be seen at an old palace in Mexico City that is now a big museum and shop. Tourists often do all their souvenir shopping there. Or they may come just to look around, to study examples of the kind of articles they will be offered in the other towns they visit. They learn that a particular shade of blue-and-white pottery is made in Puebla, for example, and that black pottery comes from Oaxaca. They are told that the best silverware and jewelry in the country is made in the beautiful old town of Taxco (*tas*-co).

Mexico Welcomes Tourists

The visitors who come to Mexico every year, from all around the world, have made the tourist industry one of the country's largest. It is second only to petroleum as a source of income.

The tourist industry has created jobs for the thousands of construction workers employed to build new hotels in cities, and transform tiny coastal villages into international vacation resorts. It has put other thousands of Mexicans to work to staff those hotels and resorts, and to provide service in shops, gas stations and restaurants, on airlines, buslines, and trains.

Tourists also employ the Mexicans who can guide them among ancient Indian ruins, explain the ritual of a bullfight in Mexico City's big bullring, or share their knowledge of a traditional Mexican fiesta.

The fiestas that take place in Mexico, almost every day of the year, are popular tourist attractions. But they are not "shows" put on for strangers. They are a very real part of life in every corner of the country.

Sometimes the main event of a village fiesta is a game of baseball or soccer, both very popular sports in Mexico. Or it may be a

*Pageantry and ritual are an
important part of every bullfight.*

jaripeo, a combination of small-town rodeo and small-town bull-fight.

Some of Mexico's fiestas, however, are famous throughout the land and are often on a tourist's list of things that must be seen. Among them are several events that celebrate a Christian religious holiday and also preserve an ancient Indian tradition. One of these is the Corpus Christi fiesta in Papantla (pa-*pan*-tla), in the state of Veracruz.

Corpus Christi Thursday, a Catholic feast day, is marked throughout Mexico by a special mass. But in Papantla and in several other towns it is the occasion for the remarkable Indian dance called the Dance of the Flyers, performed from the top of a high pole.

The pole, a tall straight tree that has been cut and stripped of its branches, is set up in the town square. A revolving cap is fitted to the top of the pole, and a small square frame is attached to the cap. Then four ropes, each long enough to reach the ground, are wound around the pole near its top. When it is time for the performance, four dancers and a musician climb to the top of the pole by means of vine ladders.

Each dancer ties the end of one of the ropes around his waist and seats himself on the frame. The musician takes his place on the revolving cap, not much bigger than a large pot lid, and begins to dance while he plays his flute and his drum.

At a given signal the four dancers throw themselves off the frame, head down. While the platform revolves, they spin downward as their ropes unwind. At the last moment, as they are nearing the ground, they turn somersaults and land on their feet.

Tourists held spellbound by this spectacle usually depend on their Mexican guides to tell them about its source. The guides explain that the dance was performed centuries ago by the Aztecs, and that the four dancers were expected to reach the ground in exactly thirteen revolutions of the platform. The number of revolutions, multiplied by the number of dancers—fifty-two revolutions altogether—represented the fifty-two-year cycle of the Aztec calendar. And a good guide reminds tourists that the famous Aztec stone calendar may be seen in Mexico City's great Museum of Anthropology.

The "Single Path" of Government

In a recent poll, when Mexicans were asked what they most blamed for the fact that Mexico hasn't had "the progress it deserves," more than a third of them put the blame on "bad government." But they have had the same kind of government for over half a century, and are not likely to change it. Mexico is the most stable country in Latin America—the only one which has not had a revolution during the past fifty years.

Since 1929 Mexico has been ruled by a single political party always spoken of as the PRI. The letters are the initials of its Spanish name, *Partido Revolucionario Institucional,* or Institutional Revolutionary Party. Other small parties do exist, but the PRI has elected every national president since 1929, almost all members of the national congress, and the governors of each of Mexico's twenty-nine states. For that reason many people say voting is useless, since the winners are known ahead of time. Only half the voters went to the polls in a recent election.

People who nevertheless approve of Mexico's "single path" political system, as they call it, might explain their approval in words like these: "The government must be able to make long-range plans, carry them out, and correct any mistakes that occur along the way. It could not do this if control were handed back and forth every few years from one party to another. So we think it is best to leave the government in the hands of the PRI."

Mexican law permits a president to serve only one term, but he has great authority during the six years he is in office. He "decides what shall be done, by whom, when, and how," as one expert put it.

One of his important duties is to choose, after consulting other PRI officials, the candidate who the party will support to succeed him in office. Government officers and industrialists always try to guess ahead of time who his choice will be. Guessing correctly, and winning the favor of the next president, may ensure their own success and good fortune during the next six years.

Usually the candidate selected is one of the president's cabinet ministers, or someone else high in the government. He may not be well known to the public. But once his name has been announced, he tours the country so that people may see him and hear him speak.

In 1981, for example, President José López Portillo announced that his Minister for Planning and Budget, Miguel de la Madrid Hurtado, would be the PRI's candidate for the July 1982 elections. Mexicans who knew little about the candidate soon learned that he held a master's degree in public administration from Harvard University, that he was the president's close friend, and that he was believed to be the best person to carry forward the president's economic and political policies.

Mexico's capital is its most important city as well as its largest. Its streets are clogged with traffic and noisy with honking horns. Thousands of people must travel two hours or more to get to work and back home again. Mexico City has a subway, but it doesn't yet extend to all the suburbs, so most commuters use their own cars or take busses. Gasoline fumes from thousands of such vehicles, along with dust and the smoke from surrounding factories, form a yellowish haze that usually hides the snow-crested mountains towering above the city. Despite the continuous building of new large apartment houses, there is a shortage of good housing even for fam-

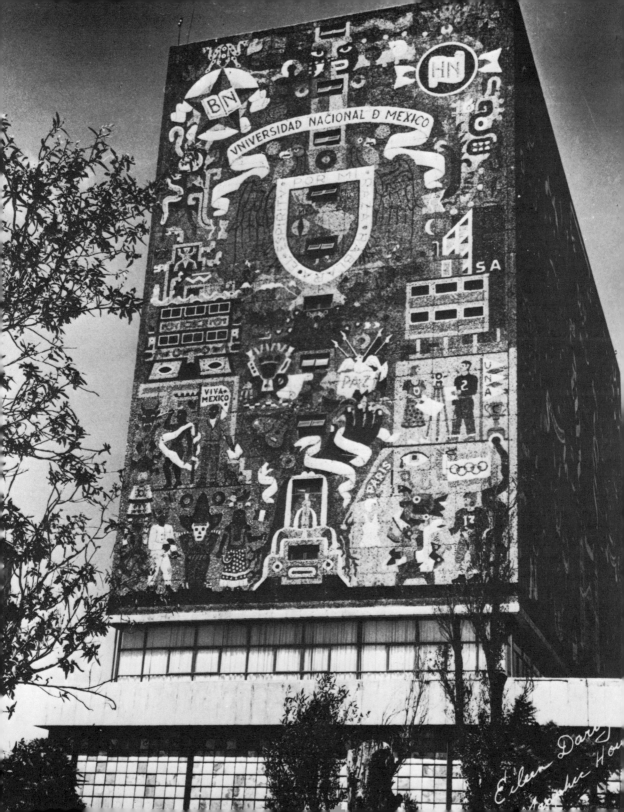

ilies able to pay high rents. And the city's miserable slums grow larger and more crowded every year.

But Mexico City does have splendid museums and art galleries, theaters and concert halls, and parks. It has the magnificent National University of Mexico, founded in 1551 and one of the two oldest universities in the Western hemisphere. It has shops and restaurants of every kind. Most important of all, it has the offices of a government that controls or touches in some way almost everything that happens throughout the country.

Mexicans know that living in their capital is often difficult, unpleasant, and uncomfortable. But many of them insist they would not want to live—they could not imagine living—anywhere but in the city they call, simply, Mexico.

The colorful library of the
National University of Mexico
is imaginatively decorated.

Mexico Looks North and South — and Ahead

Mexico entered the 1980s with the power and prestige of an oil-rich nation. It could meet on a new footing with its neighbor to the north, because the United States was among the countries eager to buy Mexican oil and natural gas. It could influence its smaller neighbors to the south—the countries of Central America—by giving them financial and technical assistance. It sold them oil at a special low price, for example, made them generous loans, and reduced import duties on the goods they had to sell.

Mexico's president also conducted a newly active foreign policy in and around the whole Caribbean region. He maintained openly friendly relations with Communist Cuba. He supported the leftist regime of Nicaragua. He encouraged such revolutionary groups as the guerrillas of El Salvador, then attempting to overthrow their government.

President José López Portillo's first meeting with newly-elected President Ronald Reagan was important for both countries. At its end, both men said their talks had been friendly and helpful. And their respect for each other did suggest that the serious differences between their countries could become a thing of the past.

But, in fact—and to no one's surprise—the two men had not reached solutions to two major problems. One was the illegal immigration each year of thousands of Mexicans into the United States. The other was the unsettled political situation in much of the Caribbean region.

Both presidents knew that unemployed Mexicans in search of work could easily cross the border into the United States. The Rio Grande which separates Mexico from Texas is unguarded for most of its length. And United States employers were willing to hire those "wet backs," as they are often called, because the Mexicans would accept low-paid menial jobs that most Americans refused.

Both presidents also knew that if the illegal immigrants were rounded up and deported, or if the border were better guarded to prevent their crossing, Mexico's millions of unemployed could threaten its government's stability. This was a possibility that President Portillo did not want to face. President Reagan, too, hoped to avoid it; he did not want to see an unstable government, or possibly a workers' revolt, just beyond the southern border of the United States.

The other problem, concerning the Caribbean region, arose out of strongly differing policies. United States policy was that leftist governments and leftist anti-government revolutionists in that region were pawns in the power struggle between communism and the Western democracies, because they received aid from the Soviet Union by way of Cuba. The United States therefore supported those who fought the leftists.

Mexico's policy was that "leftists" came into being as a result of poverty, or lack of civil rights, or both. It was not because they wished to ally themselves with the Soviet Union, but that they would accept help in their struggle from anyone willing to give it—and that help had come most often through Communist Cuba.

But now, President Portillo told President Reagan, Mexico could serve as a neutral source of that aid. This would mean the political upheavals in the region would no longer have to be part of the worldwide East-West power struggle. It could mean the beginning of a new stability for the whole area. And he soon thereafter offered himself as an intermediary between the United States, on the one hand, and Cuba and the revolutionary groups on the other. American officials were wary of the offer, but it was not refused outright.

During the months after that first meeting between the two presidents, all Mexican-American problems were intensified by the increasingly serious economic recession that struck most industrialized countries in the early 1980s. Construction projects came to a halt. Factories slowed their output or closed altogether, thus reducing the industrial demand for oil. Consumers, at the same time, had begun to conserve oil and were using less of it.

The result, in 1981, was called an "oil glut": the oil-producing nations had more oil on hand than they could sell, even after they reduced their prices.

Mexico's income from oil fell sharply. Government plans for expanding oil refineries and building new ports were postponed or abandoned. Thousands of Mexicans lost their jobs. Thousands more, in search of work, came to realize they had little hope of finding it.

The number of illegal immigrants into the United States increased. And they met increasing resentment from Americans who were also out of work and who felt that all jobs—even poorly paid ones—should belong to them. The American government set up new and more stringent programs to round up illegal immigrants and send them back home.

Mexico's problems for the near future—and perhaps far into the twenty-first century— will probably be the same ones the country has faced for many years: too many Mexicans lacking decent housing, good schools, and medical care; too many living in poverty either from lack of land or lack of jobs.

The programs supported by oil profits, and designed to help Mexicans achieve a better life, were cut back or halted when those profits declined. They will be restored as soon as the widespread recession ends and the country's income increases, Mexico's economists and social planners say.

But many of those experts also say that so long as Mexico's population continues to grow at its present high rate, there will never be enough land or jobs to provide a good life for everyone. Controlling population growth, those people insist, is the single biggest challenge that Mexico faces as its government and its people look ahead into the future.

Index